Chords for Mandolin, Irish Banjo, Bouzouki

Tenor Mandola
Mandocello

by John Loesberg

Easy Chords in all keys,
with sections on tunings,
capos and chord-relations

OSSIAN

Explanation of chord diagrams

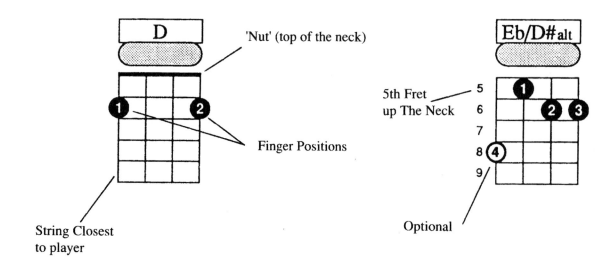

D

'Nut' (top of the neck)

Finger Positions

String Closest to player

Eb/D#alt

5th Fret up The Neck — 5
6
7
8
9

Optional

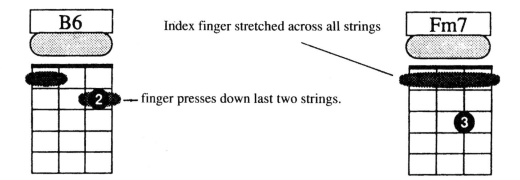

B6

Index finger stretched across all strings

2 — finger presses down last two strings.

Fm7

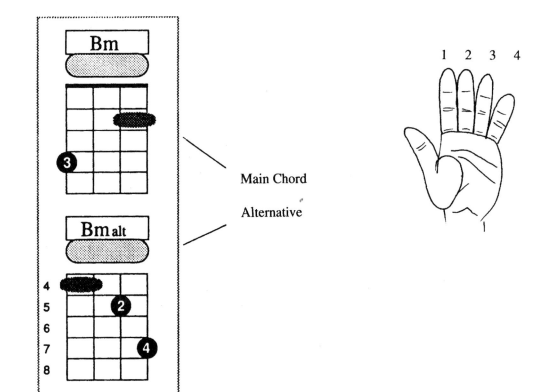

Bm

Main Chord

Alternative

1   2   3   4

Bmalt

4
5
6
7
8

Mandolin

All chords are given as suitable for mandolin and traditional Irish banjo tuning. G — D — A — E (standard fiddle tuning).

Bouzouki

Use the same chords as for mandolin. The bouzouki is tuned an octave lower — so that all chords will also sound an octave below.

Standard Banjo & (Tenor) Mandola

Also known as viola tuning, (C — G — D — A) which is 5 tones lower than mandolin tuning. In order to keep the chord-diagrams uncluttered only the mandolin chord name is given. But just below it a space is provided for a 'translation' into standard banjo or Mandola chord symbols.

Mandolin Tuning:	C	C#/Db	D	D#/Eb	E	F	F#/Gb	G	G#/Ab	A	Bb	B
Standard Banjo/Mandola Tuning:	F	F#/Gb	G	G#/Ab	A	Bb	B	C	C#/Db	D	D#/Eb	E

Examples:

Mandolin Chord	Dm	becomes	Gm
Mandolin Chord	F7sus4	becomes	Bbsus4
Mandolin Chord	Adim	becomes	Ddim

Mandocello

Use the same chords as for the standard Banjo & Tenor Mandola.
The Mandocello is tuned an octave below this.
An alternative tuning for the mandocello is an octave below mandolin tuning.

To Change Keys:

The keys used in sheetmusic and songbooks are frequently those which will suit the composer or performer him/herself. Often a key right for one singer may cause somebody else to force the voice into a squeak or groan. There is a certain amount of change possible without too much fuss (with the use of a capo in up to four or five different positions on the neck) but on the whole it pays off the extra effort to learn how to change the key without the use of a capo. This is called 'transposing a key' and gives access to accompaniments either lower or higher in sound than originally printed. Once understood any song in any songbook may be tailored to suit your voice.

KEYS ARE IN MAJOR OR MINOR

The most important keys available are:

A	B	C	D	E	F	G	(MAJOR KEYS)
Am	Bm	Cm	Dm	Em	Fm	Gm	(MINOR KEYS)

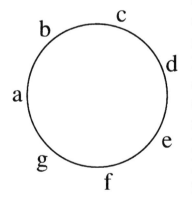

When a key is found to be unsuitably high or low, use the clock on this page to find a better one; turn CLOCKWISE to get a HIGHER sound, ANTI-CLOCKWISE to go down. After having chosen a new key, look at the tables on the next page and locate the old key as indicated on your sheetmusic or songbook, under the MAJOR or MINOR section and pick out the chords in the song from the column of chords directly DOWN FROM THE KEYCHORD. The twelve chords under this KEYCHORD are the most likely ones to appear in the average folk or popsong. The equivalent of the old chords in the NEW KEY can now be located simply by moving SIDEWAYS towards the column of the NEW KEY.

KEY AND KEYCHORD:	A	B	C	D	E	F	G
	D	E	F	G	A	Bb	C
	E	F#	G	A	B	C	D
	F#m	G#m	Am	Bm	C#m	Dm	Em
	E7	F#7	G7	A7	B7	C7	D7
	A7	B7	C7	D7	E7	F7	G7
	Bm	C#m	Dm	Em	F#m	Gm	Am
	C#m	Ebm	Em	F#m	G#m	Am	Bm
	Em	F#m	Gm	Am	Bm	Cm	Dm
	G	A	Bb	C	D	Eb	F
	B	C#	D	E	F#	G	A
	B7	C#7	D7	E7	F#7	G7	A7
	D7	E7	F7	G7	A7	Bb7	C7

ASSOCIATED CHORDS

KEY AND KEYCHORD:	Am	Bm	Cm	Dm	Em	Fm	Gm
	Dm	Em	Fm	Gm	Am	Bbm	Cm
	D7	F#7	G7	A7	B7	C7	D7
	G	A	Bb	C	C	Eb	F
	Em	F#m	Gm	Am	Bm	Cm	Dm
	C	D	Eb	F	G	G#	Bb
	D	E	F	G	A	Bb	C
	E	F#	G	A	B	C	D
	F	G	G#	Bb	C	C#	Eb
	Bm	C#m	Dm	Em	F#m	Gm	Am
	F#m	G#m	Am	Bm	C#m	Dm	Em
	C#m	Ebm	Em	F#m	G#m	Am	Bm
	B7	C#7	D7	E7	F#7	G7	A7

ASSOCIATED CHORDS

N.B. The chords associated with each key are not in the order as is usual in musical theory: they reflect more or less in order of importance the likelihood of their appearance in the average folk- or pop-song.

   #'s are called sharps and raise the pitch of your chord by a semitone (one box, or fret).

   b's stand for flats and lowers the chord a semitone.

Chord Relationships

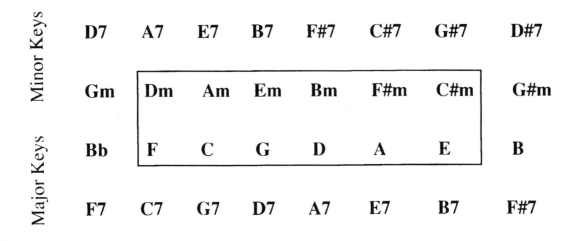

Minor Keys	D7	A7	E7	B7	F#7	C#7	G#7	D#7
Minor Keys	Gm	Dm	Am	Em	Bm	F#m	C#m	G#m
Major Keys	Bb	F	C	G	D	A	E	B
Major Keys	F7	C7	G7	D7	A7	E7	B7	F#7

Example
The Related chords in the key of C major:

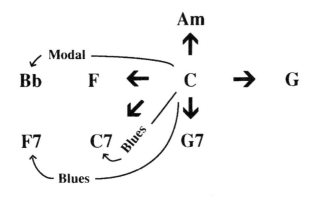

Example
The Related chords in the key of A minor:

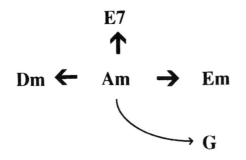

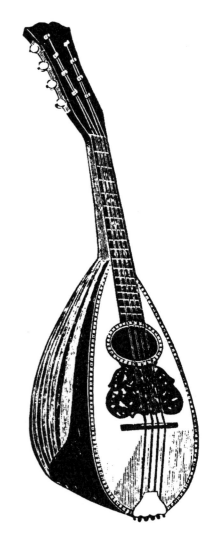

Use of Capo

Key changes can also be effected by using a CAPO (CAPO D'ASTRA). The idea is to play easy chord-shapes higher up the neck by making the strings a little shorter, using a clamp-type device that presses down on all six strings in any position required.
The pitch of all six strings is raised by attaching the capo in any of the first four or five boxes (space between two frets), clamped down just in front of a fret. The advantages are numerous : just by fixing the capo in the first box (just in front of the first metal fret) and while physically playing chords in the key of A minor, the actual pitch has been raised to B flat minor, a key that would involve some finger-breaking chord-chapes if played without the capo. There's no cheating in using a capo, the advantages are too great not to use it.

Capo-transposition

CHORDS, NORMALLY IN THE KEY OF:

	A	Am	C	D	Dm	E	Em	G
With Capo in 1st Box	Bb	Bbm	C#	Eb	Ebm	F	Fm	G#
2nd Box	B	Bm	D	E	Em	F#	F#m	A
3rd Box	C	Cm	Eb	F	Fm	G	Gm	Bb
4th Box	C#	C#m	E	F#	F#m	G#	G#m	B
5th Box	D	Dm	F	G	Gm	A	Am	C

As a rule, keys like Bbm (B flat minor), Bm, Em, C#m (C sharp minor), are usually obtained by using the key and chords of Am with a capo fastened in the appropriate box.
Fm, F#m, Gm, G#m derive from Em shapes
With Major keys, A gives access to Bb and B.
C to C#, D to Eb, F to F# and G to G#.

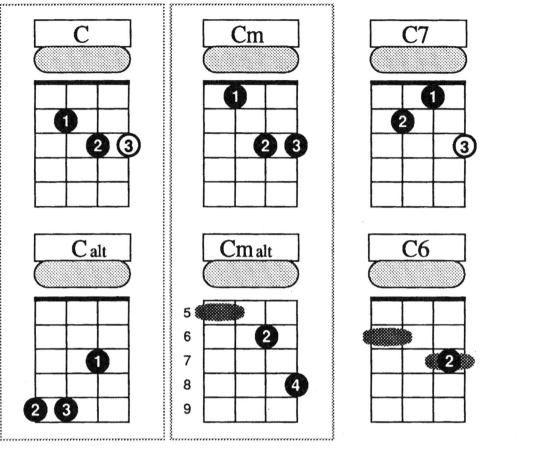

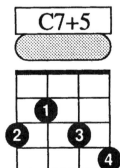

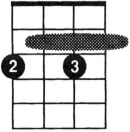

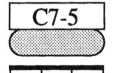

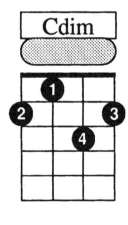

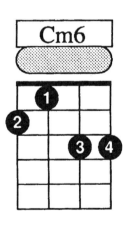

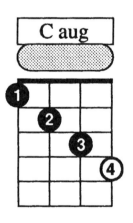

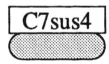

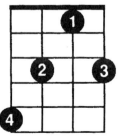

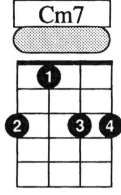

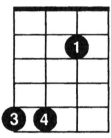

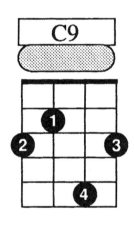

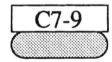

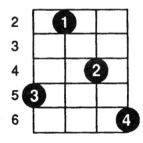

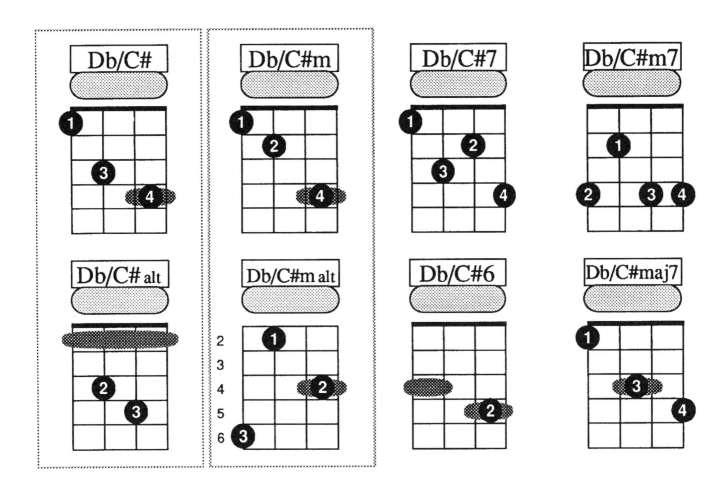

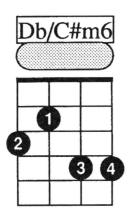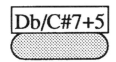 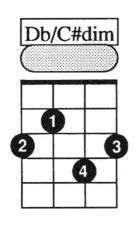 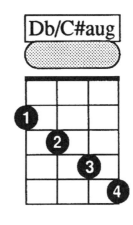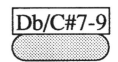 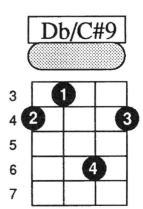

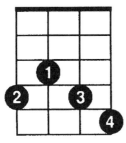 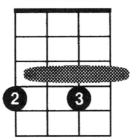 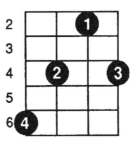 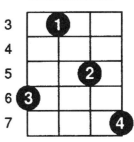

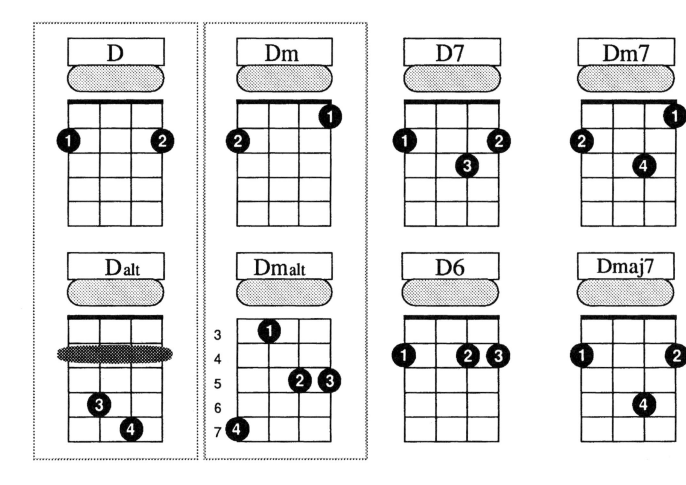

D   Dm   D7   Dm7   Dalt   Dmalt   D6   Dmaj7

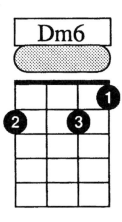
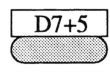
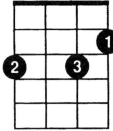

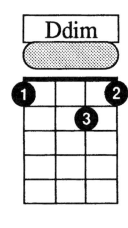

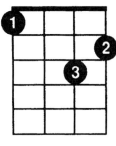

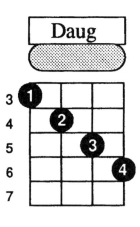

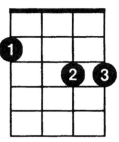

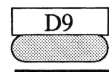
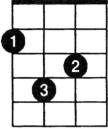
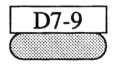
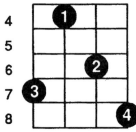

Dm6   Ddim   Daug   D9   D7+5   D7-5   D7sus4   D7-9

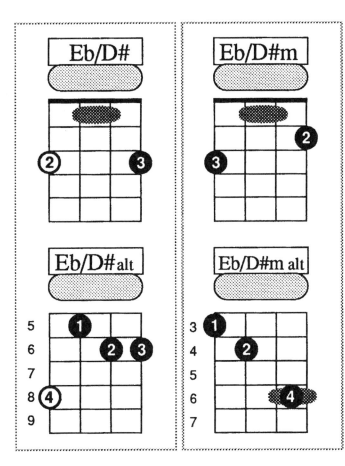

Eb/D#
Eb/D#m
Eb/D#7
Eb/D#m7

Eb/D#alt
Eb/D#m alt
Eb/D#6
Eb/D#maj7

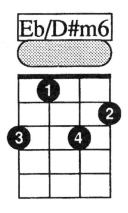
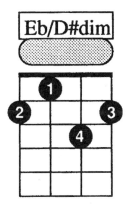
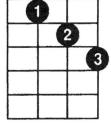
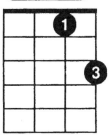

Eb/D#m6
Eb/D#dim
Eb/D#aug
Eb/D#9

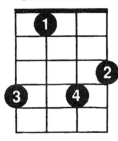
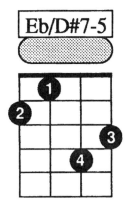
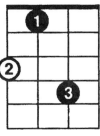
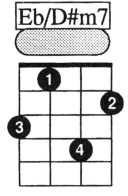

Eb/D#7+5
Eb/D#7-5
Eb/D#7sus4
Eb/D#7-9

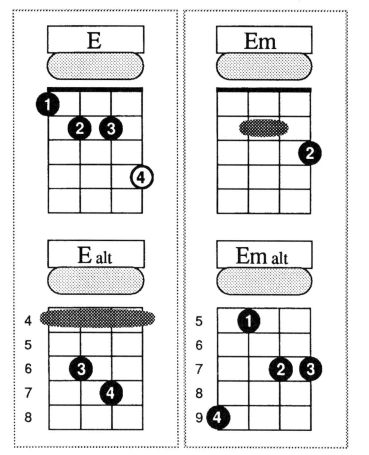

E	Em	E7	Em7

E alt	Em alt	E6	Emaj7

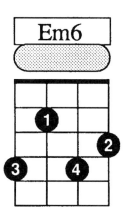 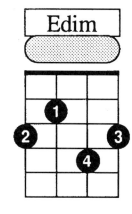 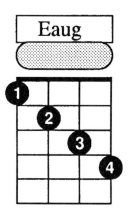 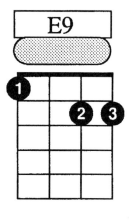

Em6	Edim	Eaug	E9

E7+5	E7-5	E7sus4	E7-9

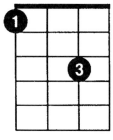 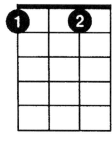 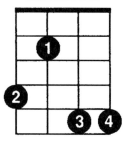 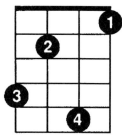

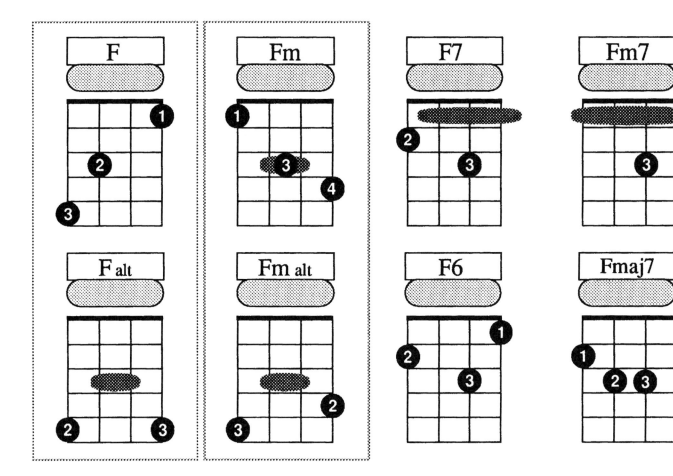

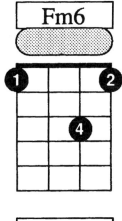
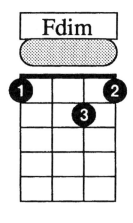
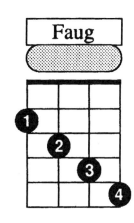
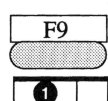
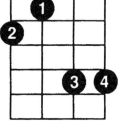

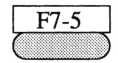
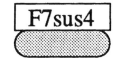
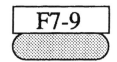

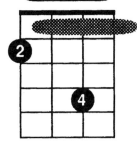
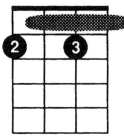
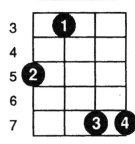
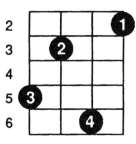

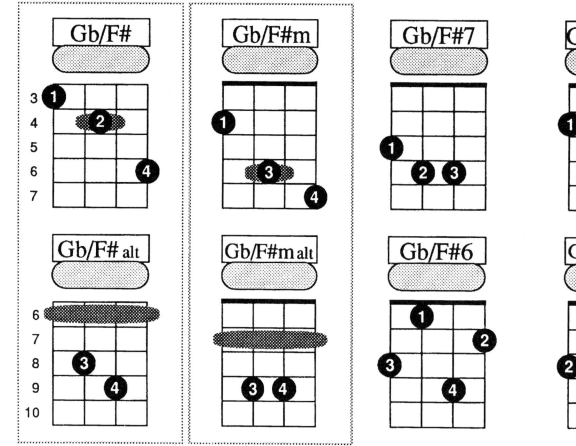

Gb/F#	Gb/F#m	Gb/F#7	Gb/F#m7

Gb/F# alt	Gb/F#m alt	Gb/F#6	Gb/F#maj7

Gb/F#m6	Gb/F#dim	Gb/F#aug	Gb/F#9

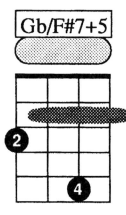
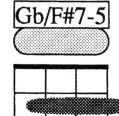
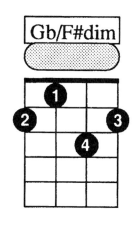
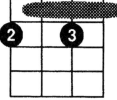

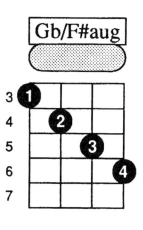
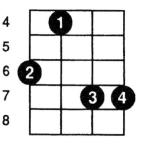
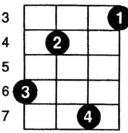
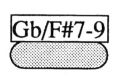
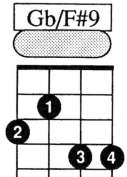
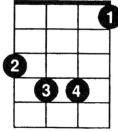

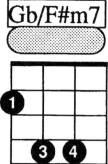
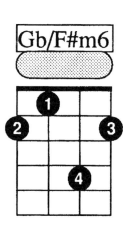

Gb/F#7+5	Gb/F#7-5	Gb/F#7sus4	Gb/F#7-9

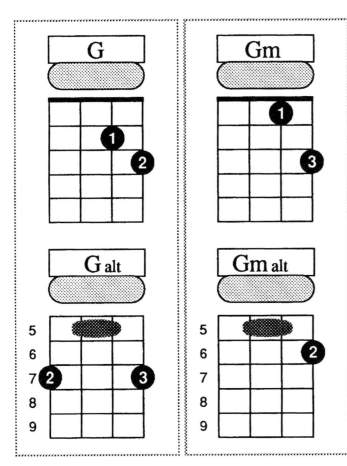
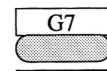
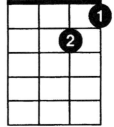
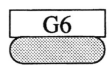
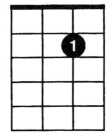
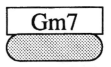

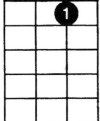
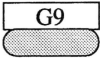
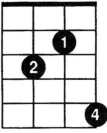
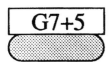
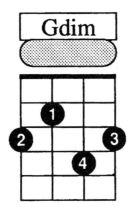
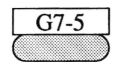
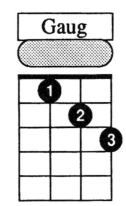
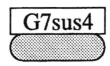
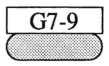
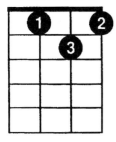
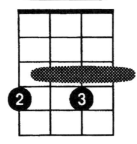
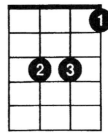
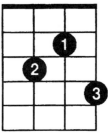

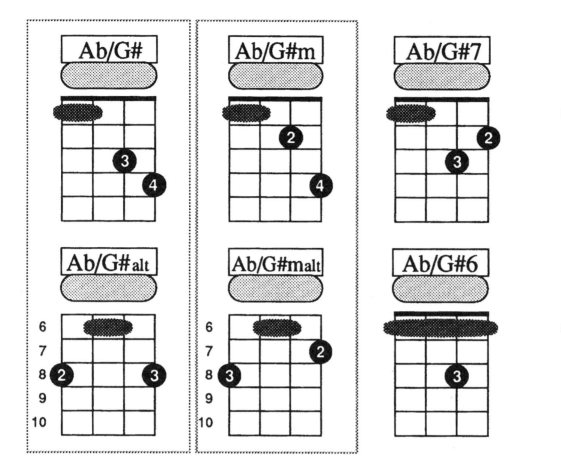

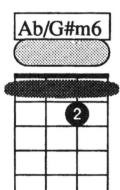

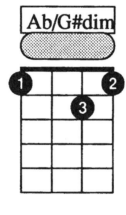

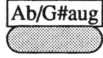

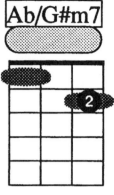

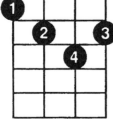

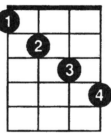

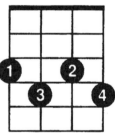

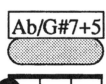

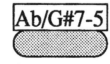

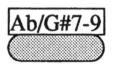

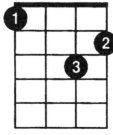

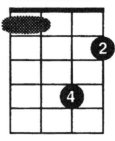

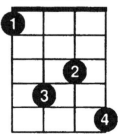

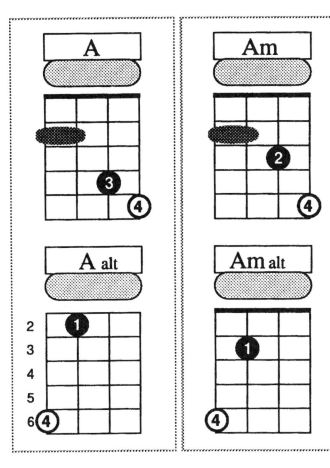

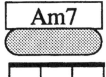 A7

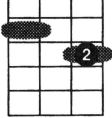 Am7
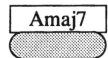

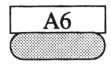 A6
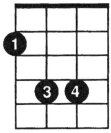

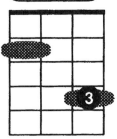 Amaj7

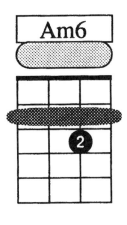 Am6
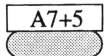

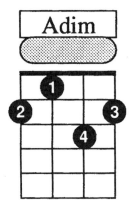 Adim

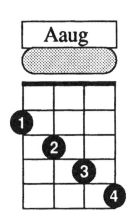 Aaug

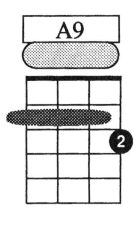 A9
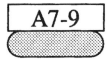

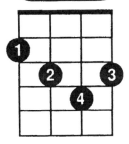 A7+5

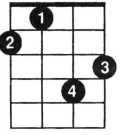 A7-5

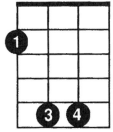 A7sus4
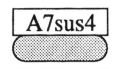

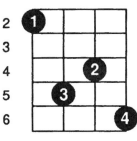 A7-9

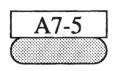

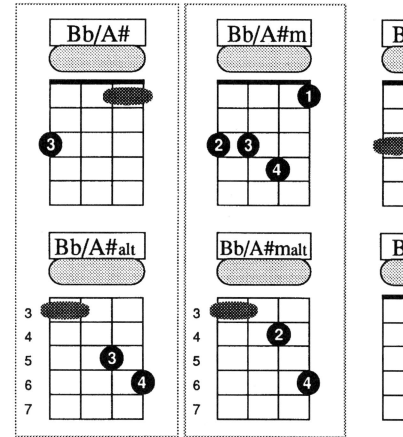

Bb/A# Bb/A#m Bb/A#7 Bb/A#m7

Bb/A#alt Bb/A#malt Bb/A#6 Bb/A#maj7

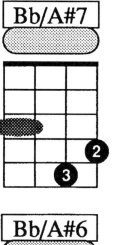
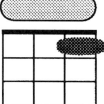

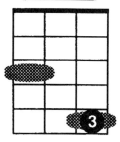
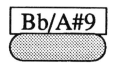
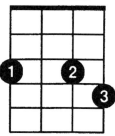
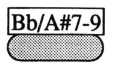

Bb/A#m6
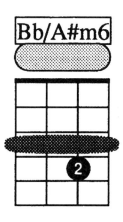
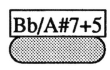
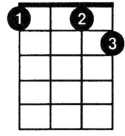

Bb/A#dim
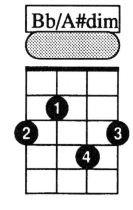
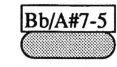
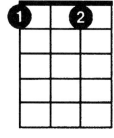

Bb/A#aug
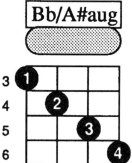
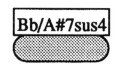
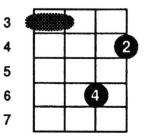

Bb/A#9

Bb/A#7+5

Bb/A#7-5

Bb/A#7sus4
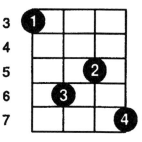

Bb/A#7-9

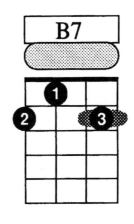

B

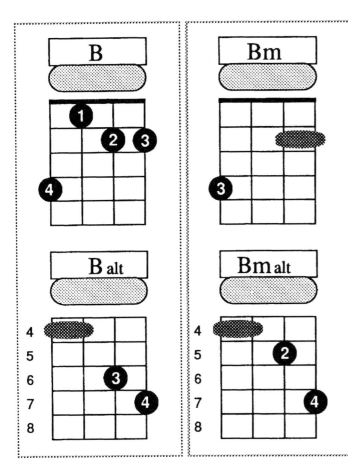

Bm

B7

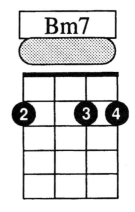

Bm7

B alt

Bm alt

B6

Bmaj7

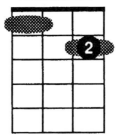

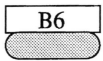

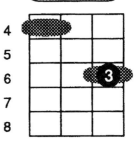

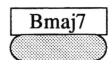

Bm6

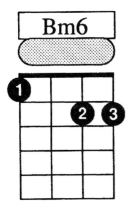

Bdim

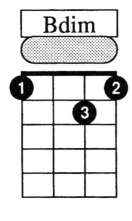

Baug

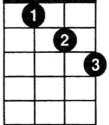

B9

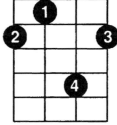

B7+5

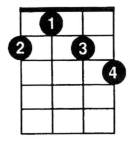

B7-5

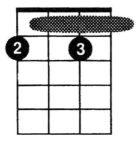

B7sus4

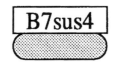

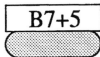

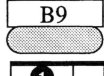

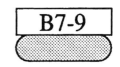

B7-9

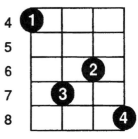

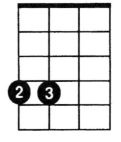

Printed in EU.

www.halleonard.com

Diagrams by Seton, Bantry.

Hal Leonard Europe Limited
Distribution Centre Newmarket Road
Bury St Edmunds Suffolk, IP33 3YB www.halleonard.com

OMB 61
ISBN 0 946005 478